Picture of a Time

Mike Armstrong

LittleLightBooks

Picture of a Time

Copyright ©2006 by Mike Armstrong

All rights reserved. No part of this book may be used or reproduced in any manner whatsoever without written permission except for quotations for articles or reviews. Printed in the United States of America. For information address Little Light Books, 5268G Nicholson Lane #122, Kensington, MD 20895.

Library of Congress Control Number: 2006908789

ISBN 0-9789894-0-6
www.littlelightshop.com

Dedicated to the august Queen,

her Child King,

their gift Christine

who wears my ring.

Intro

A good poem paints a picture
with just its words alone.
A good picture has within it
a poetry of its own.

A world of love and meaning
can be caught in a single rhyme.
Each day can be lived like a poem
when seen as a small lifetime.

A scribble here, a doodle there
it will be well worth my while,
if we meet between these lines
and both leave with a smile.

Sneak Peek

Picture of a Time..................................9
The Child King 10
The Tent...11
The Daydreamer 12
Moonrise Cafe 14
Bedtime Story.....................................17
Where Do You Go? 18
A Rainy Day at the Zoo 20
We Are Boys......................................22
Precious Jewels...................................23
The Mailbox 24
Postage Stamp Painter 25
My Tree House in the Rain 26
Scary Stories 28
Star Sailor...30
The Perfect Gift 32
The Pocket Watch................................33
Summer Days in Centerfield 34
What Color I Am..................................36
The Two Dollar Bill 37
18 Holes...39
Ivory Keys 41
Sleepfighter 42
The Hammock....................................44
In Defense of Non-Sense 45
Glenmont's Garage 46

How Hearts Break.........................48
My Little Baby Things......................49
The Ghost on Wiseman Road 50
Perfect Game...........................52
The Second Wind 54
Memory Box...........................55
My Favorite Things........................56
The Lemonade Stand.......................58
The Greeting Card 60
The Number One Rule When Riding the Bus............ 61
The Twelfth and Final Round 62
My Shoe Box..........................64
Proper Greeting 65
The Day My Goldfish Died 66
The 'Brella 68
What Boys Live By 70
Dressing Myself 71
"When I Was a Kid".......................72
The Thing Behind the Door....................73
The Homestretch 74
Headshaker! 76
The Orange Crayon....................... 77
The Backyard 78
Did You Tell Your Mom Not to Worry Today? 80

Twenty-Six Bricks

Twenty-Six Bricks 83
The Scribbler 84
Discovery 85
What's it all Mean? 86
"To Do" List 88
Let's Write a Poem 89
Think Better 90
For Lease 91
George's Typewriter 92
What a Writer Knows Best 94
The Loveliest Couple 95
The Little Girl Who Eats Her Words 96
What Was Left on the Ground 98
A Poem is a Little Child 99
Big Words 100
I See a Story... 101
Help Me End This Poem 102

Other Things

Other Things. 105
The Why-Nots. 106
What's in Your Safe?. 107
How High You Can Go 108
Angel Sight. 109
Something Lost. 110
Poor Clare. 111
My Financial Planner 112
The Right Time. 113
The Way Things Happen 114
The Dangers of a Well-Fed-Big-Head 116
Put Together Right 118
The Ballad of Wasted Time 119
Beneath Her Mantle 120
St. Michael's Army 121
Hidden Gold. 122
A Little Advice 123
Everyone's Missing Something. 124
Daring. 126
Glimmers 127
Summer of the August Queen. 128
Christmas Song. 130
The Picture Comes Clearer 131

Picture of a Time

I have a picture in my head of a time
but I'm not sure which one.
It was a time of adventure
and wild, carefree fun.
It was before we got smart
and our spirits got old,
when there was simple truth inside
the stories we told.
And the verses we heard
had the sound of a song,
while our hearts leapt for heaven
because our love was so strong.
And life was a dare —
we spit at our fears.
And laughing at ourselves
saved so many tears.
Although I am young
I can picture a time
when stories had morals
and poems would rhyme.

The Child King

There is the child who is running free,
exploring her backyard.
She sees things all the world can't see,
she's never standing guard.

There is the child waiting to capture
a hero in his eyes.
He'll give the honor, as children do,
to the one who simply tries.

There is the child who hasn't been told
her years are just a sum.
That picture of faith in the child's heart
is what she must become.

There is a Child who is a King,
and will forever be.
He holds the whole world in His hands —
please speak to Him of me.

The Tent

We pull the cover up over the tent,
we're as safe as safe can be.
We huddle in warmth, pure heaven-sent,
my brother, sister and me.

We hide from the world for just a spell
in our cove of stories and dreams.
Where is our tent? We'll never tell,
a secret in stitches and seams.

A magical den that can only be seen
by eyes inside of its door.
Suspended in time and floating between
the moon and my bedroom floor.

The Daydreamer

As I sit here in class, my mind begins to wander
off into the depths of the wild, blue yonder.
History — just words running through my head,
my pencil in hand like five pounds of lead.

I'm thinking of beaches, oceans and lakes.
I'm thinking of what funny turns my life takes.
I'm thinking of the sound the strong wind makes.
I'm thinking of my joys, worries, heartaches.

I'm thinking of a present wrapped in ribbon and bow.
I'm thinking of the winter, the cold and the snow.
I'm thinking of all the things one person could know.
I'm thinking of how good I feel, and after, how low.

I'm thinking of all the people for whom I care.
I'm thinking of a laugh, a thrill and a scare.
I'm thinking of all the things I could do if I dared.
I'm thinking of it all behind a blank stare.

I'm thinking of religion, my faith and my God.
I'm tired and I'm sleepy, my head begins to nod.
Through five more minutes of class I must plod.
So many other things to think about —
doesn't it seem odd?

As the bell rings, the teacher calls out my name.
Back to reality — it's just not the same.
"What were you thinking today?"
she asks with concern.
Her voice is so sharp, her expression so stern.

"Of life, the heavens and nature!" I want to say.
"Nothing," I answer and go on my way.

Moonrise Cafe

Each summer evening when the sun
does shine that final ray,
the cooler breezes call us out
to our cool, sidewalk cafe.

The doors swing open to our hearts,
we talk about our day.
No judges sit upon a bench
in our outdoor cafe.

We let it fly, the good and bad,
no rules for what we say.
No walls confine our sharing meal
at our moonrise cafe.

Bedtime Story

Tell me a bedtime story,
make it something good,
about a trip to 1600
in a time machine of wood.

Tell me of a far-off place,
an island lost in mist.
Tell me of a noble prince
and the princess that he kissed.

Tell me of a valiant warrior
and the giant that he slew.
Tell me of some nice, old elves
and ghosts and goblins, too.

Tell me a bedtime story
to dance inside my head
and bring me dreams of wonder
while an angel guards my bed.

Where Do You Go?

Sometimes when you're

here

you're really not

there.

And your face becomes full
of the emptiest stare.

With your feet on the ground
as you float in the air...

I'd love to know where

here is

when you're there.

A Rainy Day at the Zoo

There's a place in the city to go when it rains,
when the puddles widen around city drains.
And the streams begin to run alongside every curb,
streams no dam could stop, no hand could disturb.

There's a place to meet a lion, a rhino, a bear,
from the commonest of creatures
to the exotic and rare.
They dream of their jungles,
their oceans, their plains.
They dream of their homes each day
when it rains.

When it's sunny and blue they spend their whole day
propped up on a stage, put out on display —
while ten thousand eyes
burn through their front door,
and ten thousand ears
just pray for a roar.

While five thousand mouths shout,
"Get up and go!"
And five thousand hearts
beat for a good show.

With few people there, they act like they're home.
They run, howl and swim; they fly, jump and roam.

They put on their show — the greatest on earth.
They act like they did in the land of their birth.

They love gentle souls who come out their way —
and walk the zoo
on a rainy day.

We are Boys

In forests, on hills
we build our towers.
On creeks and rivers
we fill our hours.

Hockey sticks and skates,
baseball bats and spikes,
we use to do our battle
before retreating on our bikes.

We need no audience
to make each one a star;
we win, we lose, we fall, we rise —
we're boys, that's who we are.

Precious Jewels

When the angel of sleep
finally touches your head,
she leaves a precious
face in her stead.

A treasure of mine
held deep in my heart,
a picture in time
that will never depart.

Heavy eyelids, my girl
drifts slowly away
to dream dreams of heaven —
the never-ending day.

For now night must fall
and we must say "good-night,"
and surrender our care
to our guardian's sight.

In the world fortunes fall
and fortunes may rise,
but none are as precious
as a girl's sleepy eyes.

The Mailbox

I wonder what's in the mailbox today,
you know I can't wait to look —
maybe a letter from the President,
maybe a storybook,
maybe a card
from my dearest Grandma,
maybe a greeting from Mars,
maybe a trinket from India,
maybe some jam in glass jars,
maybe a jewel from the crown
of the King of a faraway land,
maybe a note from the Pope,
written neat and in his own hand.
Maybe a piece of something
that somebody happened to see,
somewhere along their journey
that made them think of me.
Phone calls are fine,
a visit is nice
but nothing can quite compare,
to my name by a stamp
in my letter-box
sent here from the "GREAT OUT THERE!"

Postage Stamp Painter

I want to be
the postage stamp painter
so my work will never fail,
to travel to every
faraway place
that can be reached
by US Mail.

Who does that job
with canvas so tiny,
the back of which
is damp?

It takes real genius
to paint those gems
upon a postage stamp.

My Tree House in the Rain

I see a shower from where I sit,
the water pours down the drain.
I see the world as it really lay
from my tree house in the rain.

I've watched the birds, God's weathermen
fly from the windowpane,
to let me know the coming clouds
will no longer hold their rain.

I feel the rhythms of the earth
as I watch the weather vane;
a peace, a calm that man can't give
in my tree house in the rain.

Scary Stories

Was that noise the voice inside your head,
or the thing behind the door?
Did you just hear steps drawing near,
upon the creaking floor?

Have you ever seen, on Halloween,
a ghost not quite at rest?
Or the haunting trace of a sea witch's face
looming 'neath the dark wave's crest?

Is it a tale told tall about the underground ball
where the people in the gutter dance?
Or the man wrapped neat in the white linen sheet
half-alive in a curse-ed trance?

I wonder if you know about the monster of snow
who comes alive whenever it gets deep?
Or the specters that loom in your bedroom
once you have fallen asleep?

You had better listen close and take a good dose
of what I'm about to say.
You have something inside that can make monsters hide
and chase every goblin away.

Please don't be afraid, nothing has ever been made
as strong as a child's brave heart.
So give a scary a scare with your best icy glare
and give a startler a start.

Remember the night is just a day with no light,
always stand brave and true.
The King of happy endings
beats the prince of terror pending
with help from a hero like you.

Star Sailor

There is a sailor amidst the stars,
he's circling the moon.
He fuels the sun then maps out Mars,
then jump starts old Neptune.

He dodges comets and meteorites
then rides a Saturn ring.
He lights the lamps of the Northern Lights
with the candle on his wing.

There is a sailor above the sky,
he sails beyond the air.
If a shooting star might catch your eye,
you'll know that he is there.

Sailing up and sailing on
while astral songs he sings,
beyond the dusk, beyond the dawn
toward great celestial things.

The Perfect Gift

I think a ball is the perfect gift
because you need a friend to share it,
which is better than a shirt
which only takes one to wear it.

But then again a shirt,
can be given right off your back,
which is better than a coat
spending most months on a rack.

But a coat just might be better
to keep the receiver warm,
to let them know you're there
to help during the storm...

...which is better than a ball
where you need a friend to catch it
unless it comes with a dog
who would gladly run and fetch it.

I guess the best gift is the giving
which is better than a loan —
because the more of it you give
the more of it you own.

The Pocket Watch

The pocket watch tells me the spot
where our old earth has spun.
And how much more, my eyes now sore
will get to see the sun.

It begs an ear for me to hear
the story of all men,
a chime for the first Christmas time,
to mark each turn since then.

It shows me how to bless the now
with each tick of my heart.
And soldier on through dusk and dawn,
each step a brand new start.

Summer Days in Centerfield

I don't know what time it is
and I really and truly don't care.
There is nowhere else I gotta' be,
nothing nice I gotta' wear.
I don't even know what day it is,
what week or month or year.
The sun is up and it's summertime;
my summer home is right here.
Time causes so much worry
in everyone I see.
But my time is marked by innings —
by outs one, two and three.
It's summertime, I'm in centerfield,
it's where I'm supposed to be.
Leftfield's to my right and right's to my left —
it all makes sense to me.
We don't need any watches
or even one dollar bill.
'Cause money is no good here
and time is standing still.
So drive in your cars and pull out your hair
(it makes no difference to me.)
But hold all my calls, I'm shagging fly balls
and all is just how it should be!

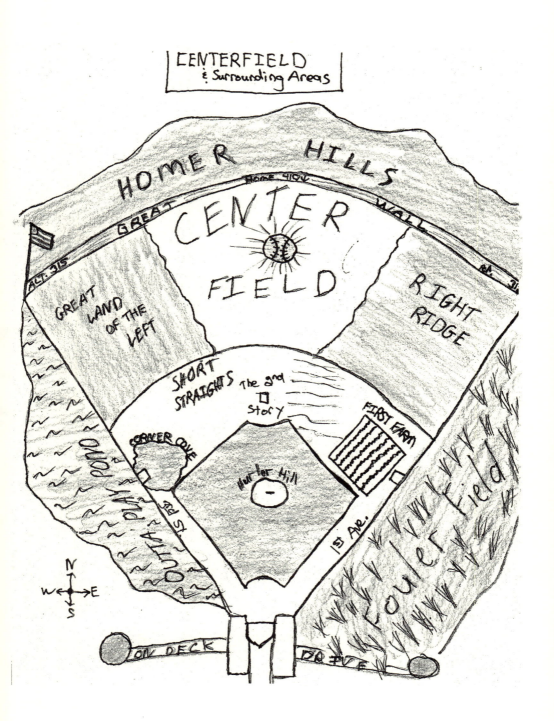

What Color I Am

If I'm red I'm embarrassed,
if I'm blue I am sad,
if I'm green then I'm jealous,
if I'm hot I am mad,
if I'm cold I'm indifferent,
if I'm white I am ill,
if I'm yellow I'm a coward,
if I'm gray I'm a pill,
if I'm black I show profit,
if I'm pink I am tickled,
if I'm gold then I'm good,
if I'm silver I've been nickeled,
if I'm dry then I'm witty,
if I'm all wet I'm a joke,
if I turn purple please help me —
I am starting to choke!

The Two Dollar Bill

I wish everything cost two bucks
like houses and toys and trucks.
My favorite bill still
is the two dollar bill.
I wish everything cost two bucks.

And I wish everybody good luck
who still has only one buck.
You will get your fill
your own two dollar bill
if you believe in hard work and good luck.

But the two dollar bill makes me see
that comfort, wealth and novelty
once had their day
but they're passing away
like the two dollar bill's destiny.

18 Holes

Here I am, an autumn morn,
leaves all orange and red.
But all I see is the short, green grass
of the putting bed.
Water waits left, a beautiful lake,
calmly asks me in.
I keep my eyes set stubbornly
upon the waving pin.
To my far out right, a sandy pit,
wants me to come and play.
But I pretend I can't hear a word
of what it has to say.
The trees ask me to take a walk
and build myself a nest.
The tall grass offers me a home
where I can take my rest.
But I drive on as I know I must,
my sticks steeled in my hand.
Through a lifetime full of traps and snares,
I navigate this land.
Can I fight on with focus strong,
dead set upon my goals,
and never quit until the end —
to conquer eighteen holes?

Ivory Keys

I have keys in my pocket
to my car and my store.
I have keys to my house
to unlock my front door.
I have keys that never leave
with me when I roam,

they are the keys to my piano —
the keys of my home.

Homes are made for music,
homes are made for fun,

so a home with a piano

is better than one with none.

Sleep Fighter

Sleep fighter, sleep fighter,
warrior of the wake,
when will you rest your head,
how long will it take?

Sleep fighter, sleep fighter,
battler of the blink,
don't you ever want to dream
or do you only want to think?

Sleep fighter, sleep fighter,
slayer of the snooze,
what do you think you'll miss,
what do you think you'll lose...

if you rest for a spell,
if you fall into a sleep,
if you close your small eyes,
if you count all your sheep?

You're a noble little warrior,
you fight with all your might;
you'll never fade out softly
into that quiet night.

Sleep fighter, sleep fighter,
the sun will rise again.
For now you fight on gamely
in a battle you can't win.

The Hammock

The hammock swings from side to side
then rests so gently still.
The hammock holds and wraps around
my body, heart and will.

I watch the sun just fade away,
I'm held above the land,
tied to higher things it swings
like a giant, loving hand.

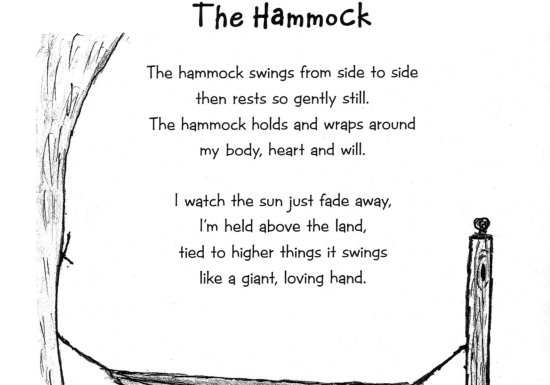

In Defense of Non-Sense

My name is nobody, how do you do?
I'm just blah-de-da-blah
and da-de-blah, too.

I'm roley-poley fun
and smartly-partly sane,
as silly-nilly words
mish-mash inside my brain.

My name is nobody, how have you done?
There is plenty of sense
in having some fun.

Glenmont's Garage

Every Sunday morning at five o'clock time,
before the sun rises up or the church bells chime.
There's a place full of wonder
that opens its doors
to the old and the young, the rich and the poor.

It's Glenmont's garage, run by Glenmont himself,
the magic of history upon every shelf.

There are pocket watches of gold
from the century before.
There are grandfather clocks
from days older than yore.

He's got a genuine six-shooter
from the old wild west,
used by "Billy the Kid" (who shot it the best.)

There's an old piece of wood
from the ark of the flood.
There are ancient gold coins
that were purchased with blood.
He'll show you an eye patch that Blackbeard wore.
There's a lesson in history in each foot of his store.

There's a piece of the sail Columbus left on shore,
next to an old-fashioned bullet from our Civil War.

There's a bottle that was used by a genie to hide
(Glenmont says there's one wish left inside.)

There are leather and wood things
now covered in dust.
There are iron and steel things
with old and new rust.

Glenmont says he has something
to remember each year —
from the beginning of time to the now and the here.

The ghosts in his garage tell me I'm never alone
while I go out and make some history of my own.

How Hearts Break

Fumbles lost on the goal line,
no-hitters lost in inning nine.
A bad decision to lose the bout,
a towering four-hundred-and-ten-foot out.
The closing horse you couldn't stop,
the two foot putt that wouldn't drop.
The rain delay on opening day,
the biggest catch that got away.
A foul called for a little tap,
a blown tire on the final lap.
When the MVP is the biggest creep,
a series lost in a four game sweep.
Your wrestler getting tied in knots,
soccer games lost on penalty shots.
But nothing could ever leave a hole,
like losing on an
overtime,
Stanley Cup final,
game 7,
arch-rival
hockey
goal.
When you play the game you accept the rule.
But God above, that's just cruel.

My Little Baby Things

I have a little baby belly
and little baby ears,
little baby eyes
for little baby tears.

A little baby smile
but no teeth in my gums,
I have one little nose
and two little thumbs.

I follow my Mommy
wherever she goes,
with my ten little fingers
and ten little toes.

I have chubby baby legs
and soft baby hair,
I study each baby part
with my best baby stare.

I see little eyelids
when I lie in my bed,
with little baby dreams
in my little baby head.

The Ghost on Wiseman Road

I have seen the ghost of Wiseman Road
pouring vinegar upon my stove.
I heard the ghost creak on my floor,
then turn and leave and shut the door.
I've known the ghost to move my things,
I've woken to the songs he sings.

I wonder if he came by flight
upon the rushing wind at night,
or through that aging wooden plank
beneath my rumbling heating tank,
or on the train that shakes my house,
or with that crawling, creeping mouse.

Perhaps he was hiding from the second-rate
music my neighbor plays way too late.
However he came, I simply know
there's a ghost down here on Wiseman Road.

Perfect Game

Twenty-seven came up,
twenty-seven went down,
never reaching first base
before leaving our town.
Our man on the mound
reared back from his knee
and struck out nine swinging
while two looked at strike three.
And two flew to right
and two popped to first
and two popped out foul
(and that's just the worst!)
Five grounded out
to our gold glove shortstop
when faced with a sinker
with plenty of drop.
One lined to left
with the crack of the wood
straight to the spot
where our leftfielder stood.
Our third baseman dove left,
our third baseman dove right
then put out a third
and then called it a night.

The last batter up
stood proud and tall
then hit a straight blast
towards our centerfield wall.
With hearts sinking fast
and eyes raised to heaven,
with split second prayers
for out twenty-seven.
Now if you were there
well, then you would know
of the great gushing wind
that began to blow
and shot with a rush
not a moment too late
from the outskirts of town
straight back to home plate.
For one night in August
we can always look back
at prayers answered neat
on the deep warning track.
Where that last ball fell safely
like a sweet drop of rain,
out twenty-seven —
one perfect game.

The Second Wind

Everyone has a second wind,
a driving energy burst.

But for you to find that second wind,
you can't quit after the first.

Memory Box

There is a memory box that sits
behind my nose,
a collection there it stores –
of scents of grass and games and trees
and salty, morning shores.

And autumn mornings,
springtime rain,
lazy, summer haze,
the smell of skies about to snow
on short-sun wintry days.

Sometimes my eyes have blinders on,
sometimes my touch sleeps numb.
Sometimes my ears just will not hear,
sometimes my voice falls dumb.

But then a smell from years gone by
will call upon its kin,
to open up childhood memories
and gladly ask me in.

My Favorite Things

As far as things of this world go,
I love it most when train whistles blow—
in the distant far-off-never-seen
behind the tree line
of evergreen.

I know of nothing surpassing in charm,
a cold, snowy evening on a Christmas tree farm
or a pumpkin patch on All Hallows' Eve
or magical stories
that children believe.

I love a diving catch
or a walk-off home run,
an overtime goal
knocking off number one.

I really love pets
and beasts in the wild.
What's better than a smile
on the face of a child?
I love rainy nights
and days by the sea,
and swinging from a tire
swinging from a tree.

I love to think of a place
where joy will not cease,
and the best gift for now
the gift of God's peace.

An unseen reminder
of a place with no pain,
like the echoing whistle
of a mysterious train.

The Lemonade Stand

I came upon three little girls selling lemonade.
I bought a cup and drank it down
and asked how much they'd made.

The first one spoke,
"We made three quarts, with plenty left in store.
So tell your friends to finish this
and gladly we'll make more."

Well it didn't take long to understand,
I'd been misunderstood.
"When I asked you what you'd made, I meant,
'Is the money good?'"

The second girl said, "It's just as good
as any money I would think —
but the lemonade, now that's the thing,
cold and fresh to drink."

"How much is all I wanted to learn-
the money you have made!"
The third girl smiled, "We have made none-
we just make lemonade."

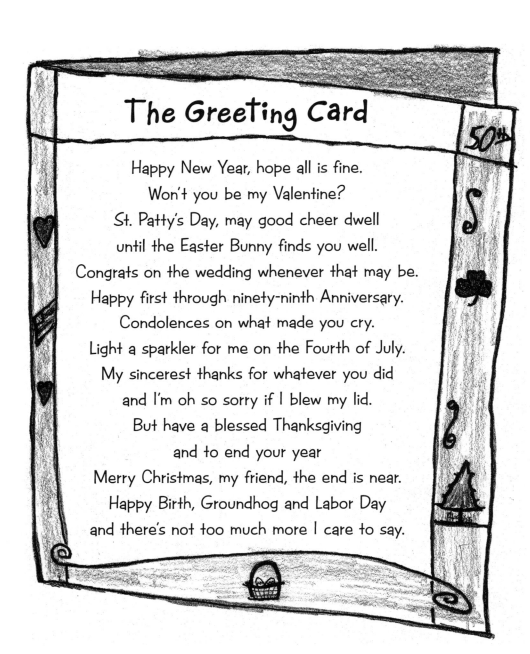

The Greeting Card

Happy New Year, hope all is fine.
Won't you be my Valentine?
St. Patty's Day, may good cheer dwell
until the Easter Bunny finds you well.
Congrats on the wedding whenever that may be.
Happy first through ninety-ninth Anniversary.
Condolences on what made you cry.
Light a sparkler for me on the Fourth of July.
My sincerest thanks for whatever you did
and I'm oh so sorry if I blew my lid.
But have a blessed Thanksgiving
and to end your year
Merry Christmas, my friend, the end is near.
Happy Birth, Groundhog and Labor Day
and there's not too much more I care to say.

The Number One Rule
When Riding the Bus

Don't spit, don't eat,
don't sing away.

Don't fight or stomp
or dance or play.

But the number one rule
when riding the bus,
that's been implored upon
each one of us:

your eyes may out the window roam...

but NEVER get off

until you're home.

The Twelfth and Final Round

Has there ever been a greater shock
than what we saw last night?
An even less expected end
than the last round of the fight?

Here our champ, our heavyweight,
there his next sure chump.
But somewhere on the road to perfect,
our legend hit a bump.

For five rounds champ did what he does,
he moved and blocked and stung.
But this time his opponent stood
when that fifth bell had rung.

Then through three more he held his lead,
though narrowing a bit.
And by round nine, the preordained
appeared less definite.

Chilling round ten, a harbinger
of horrid things to come.
A thunderous blow left our champion
sitting on his bum.

He got up quick and staggered on
determined not to fold.
By the eleventh bell our valiant hero
suddenly seemed old.

Now one day there will be surprise
when they find the "Missing Link."
And once an iceberg claimed a ship
they said God couldn't sink.

Markets crash and dynasties end,
that's how it's always been.
Man 'O War lost, the Babe struck out
even Rome took it on the chin.

But how could this have happened this way,
the twelfth round of the bout?
More unthinkable than the earth's last day-
the night champ got knocked out.

My Shoe Box

When I get some money

it goes in my bank;

nourishing food

I put in my tank.

Things with a price tag

get stored behind locks,

but things of true value

go in my shoe box.

Proper Greeting

You know you've met somebody well

if

when you've said good-byes,

they've seen your

smile,

you know their

name,

and the color of their eyes.

The Day My Goldfish Died

I know each day is blessed
but I'm glad this one is done.
My dearest, little goldfish
has seen his final sun.

He's swimming now to heaven
in the water from my eyes,
that God takes from little children
to the sea which never dries.

Where the fish from all the oceans
and the ones that graced our tanks,
swim in His sea forever
like a river with no banks.

Tomorrow I will smile again
through all the tears I've cried.
Today I'll cry that river
for my first goldfish has died.

The 'Brella

Out of my window, during the storm
I saw a strange thing by the street;
'twas a 'brella with colors
of pink, rose and red —
and four of the tiniest feet.
My glance grew to a look,
then a full blown stare,
finally revealing some more,
spilling from one side of the 'brella I spied —
a lock of curly, gold hair.
For sake of my sanity
I should cease to speak
but I must admit
(upon further inspection)
I spied a rosy cheek.
I threw open my door and
Oh! what a thing —
this four-legged, curly haired, rosy umbrella...
started to sing!
And twirl in the air
and splash near the drain,
not worrying a smidge
about blocking the rain.

I consulted my books,
I poured through my files,
found not hide nor hair
of a 'brella with smiles.
Well I shut that front door and tried to calm down,
then felt a bit forlorn.
For as soon as it came
that umbrella was gone
and left me alone with the storm.
I should have run out
and danced with the thing
and splashed and laughed 'till I cried.
How fleeting it is —
too precious to waste
by staying dry, safe and inside.

What Boys Live By

Every battle we fight is always right
except when we're dead wrong.
But either way
we'll march or play
to the beat of our own fight song.

If our cause is true
we'll ride right through
and dive right in headfirst.
If we've strayed off course
then blame the horse,
we'll march in full reverse.

Gentle ways
and peaceful days
sometimes we just don't see.

But we do know this
we'll hit or miss
in search of victory.

Dressing Myself

"I can do it," I said, as I made my stand.
I will dress myself; I don't need a hand.

I'm big enough now, I know what to do.
I know how,
I know where,
I know green,
I know blue.

I'll dress with some style, I'll dress with some tact.
How did the front of my shirt end up on my back?

And I guess my pants
have an extra leg for fun,
'cause both of my legs
fit fine in just one.

My belt's on my chest, my drawers inside out—
so I don't feel quite right, but it's not time to pout.

I'll finish the job,
I'll never retreat —
with shoes untied neatly aboard opposite feet.

"When I Was a Kid"

My mother says,"When I was a kid –
we learned our history.

It used to be we knew our dates
in their entirety."

Well forgive me, Mom, but it seems to me
there's a lot more history
than there used to be.

The Thing Behind the Door

It was late at night and there I was
lying on my bed.
The clock struck three and still no sleep,
no peace inside my head.

For there it was, framed in black,
that horrid closet door,
hiding something terrible
deep within its store.

I reached for the knob and swung it wide
holding tightly to my breath.

'Nothing' jumped out and 'Silence' roared

and scared me half to death.

The Homestretch

In a stable on a misty farm
the legends whisper still,
about a horse of strength and speed
and iron-casted will.

In the morning light while the others rest,
sometimes he can be seen –
trotting on the training oval,
his eyes still fierce and keen.

He still stands tall, his muscles peaked
and coat as black as night.
His nose still burns for finish lines,
his mind still in the fight.

In years gone by he made his name
upon the racing pitch,
in races short or distance long,
it mattered little which.

A perfect storm, a competitor
if ever one was made.
In the lead was where he made his home
and home was where he stayed.

Not fastest time nor perfect frame
was this fair champion's cry.
He simply stormed up to the front
and let no horse pass by.

Sometimes they say at the break of light,
amidst the morning frost,
you can catch a glimpse of a ghost gone by –
the horse that never lost.

Headshaker!

My father was disinclined to allow my last request.
Mom pondered my next wish
but could not acquiesce.

Even Santa wrote back that my list was declined.
And my brothers and sisters
weren't even that kind.

Is ANYONE so inclined to acquiesce or allow?
Or is the best I can get
a "yes, but not now."

When you shake your head side to side
then you frown.

Wouldn't it feel better to just nod up and down?

Headshaker! Disincliner! Non-Acquiescor!

I guess I'll just wait and ask your successor.

I'm sick of these words from my head to my toe –
why are there so many ways to say NO?!

The Orange Crayon

What if my only crayon were orange?
There are worse things that have been.
I would simply get a drawing pad
and draw a nice pumpkin.

Then I would draw a navel orange
and then a leaf in Fall,
then a glowing, setting sun,
then a basketball.

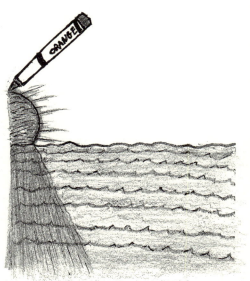

I'd draw an orange orangutan,
a Florida orange tree.
I'd draw a cone and sherbet and
all sorts of orangery.

I'd draw an orangewood violin
an orange stage I could play on.
And when I had near nothing left,
I'd draw a new orange crayon.

The Backyard

There is a place we love to go
where magical adventures grow,
like strong and towering ancient trees,
far beyond the roaring seas.

Each Saturday when the sun gives rise
to the eyelids on the children's eyes,
we set out for a land beyond –
of glistening stream and wishing pond.

We meet a snake, the worst I've seen,
a thirty foot monster all coiled and green.
And there a swing hung in the air
will take us from here to anywhere...
to escape the dungeon that lurks in back
with monsters of metal all set to attack.

But leaves are sent from the friendly trees;
they float to us on the gentle breeze,
and keep us above the growing grass,
and catch us when we fall
through the puddles' glass.

We climb the fence and see the tide
that crashes on the other side –
an endless sea both wide and long,
but our little fence keeps holding strong.

Approaching clouds swarm a sleepy sun;
no time for sleep we now must run.
For if our ally sun might lose
the darker clouds will make us choose –
between the awful water slide
and a fate still worse-
to go inside.

We stand firm, one small brave band.
We stake our claim to this wonderland.

Saturday's backyard lesson for me:

There is so much more than what we see.

Did You Tell Your Mom Not to Worry Today?

You know that is your job
because sometimes she forgets to see
the mysterious ways
that are hidden inside
of routine days.

Did you tell your Mom not to worry today?

And look up past her troubles
and trouble not with her past
and live life to its fullest
and not one bit too fast.

Did you tell your Mom not to worry today?

And look up to the huge skies
and to laugh for a moment
and to see for a moment

the world

through a child's eyes.

Twenty-Six Bricks

Twenty-Six Bricks

There are twenty-six pieces to puzzles like these.
Twenty-six bricks that fit together with ease.

You can use a brick once or a million times.
Everyone uses them (except maybe mimes.)

They come together in numerous ways.
If you choose them well
they will brighten your days.

They'll serve you like a friend
or a smart mediator.

If you use them just right
you become part creator.

There are twenty-six bricks so go have some fun.
I just used them all
except maybe one...

The Scribbler

I'll scribble on a card
or a pad
or my hand.
I'll scribble on a sidewalk
or at the beach
in the sand.
I'll scribble while I'm waiting
for the train to arrive.
When I scribble is when
I feel most alive.
I'll scribble on a napkin
while I wait for my food.
I'll scribble in a grand
or a terrible mood.
I'll scribble in my bed
before falling to sleep.
I'll scribble in my boat
sailing off to the deep.
I'll scribble about us
I'll scribble about them.
God knows I'm a scribbler –
that's just what I am.

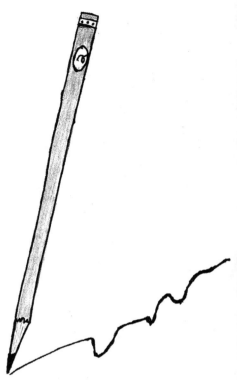

Discovery

With a bright reading light
and a good reader's look,
I spied a whole world...

inside of a book.

What's It All Mean?

"Universality" is hard to say
in almost any land.

"Ambidextrous" is difficult
to write with either hand.

"Onomatopoeia" is as confusing
as it sounds.

Spelling "obfuscation"
confuses and confounds.

A sentence using "recondite"
speaks with abstrucity.

I think I would love language
if I knew "philology."

The ambiguous "ubiquitous"
I see now everywhere.

Defining "alopecia"
will make you lose your hair.

I don't know what "equivocal" means,
but then again I do.

If I said I knew what "mendacious" meant
it wouldn't quite be true.

I uncovered the word "disinter"
and I'm so glad that I found it.

Sometimes you can figure out a word
by all the words around it.

"To Do" List

1. Make a list of things to do
2. So many things inside my head
3. A list would help me see things through
4. But I wrote this rhyme instead
5. Take a pen and paper pad
6. Label it one through ten
7. Man, this pen is acting bad
8. It wrote more rhymes instead
9. Now I'm on line number nine
10. I guess I'll try some other time...

Let's Write a Poem

Let's write a poem, what should it be —
a limerick, a ballad or verse that is free?

        How about an epic or something much neater —
        like a fourteen line sonnet in rhyme and in meter?

Should we use alliteration or a seven line septet?
How about an internal rhyme or a heroic couplet?

        Monometer, nonometer, octometer, ode?
        Pentameter that's iambic in poetic code?

Use triplets or triolets, cinquains are swell.
Compose a few rondelets and one villanelle.

        Mix in two languages for macaronic verse.
        Slant rhymes are fine, weak ones much worse.

Or how about this — write what you want to say.
Do it in your own words and in your own way.

        Then you'll always be remembered in poetic lore
        as someone who said something...
        left unsaid before.

Think Better

Learn a new word today,
the simplest thing.
The more notes you know
the better you sing.
You think in words
so the more you know,
the better you'll think,
the faster you'll grow.
The clearer you'll speak –
never to bore us.
Learn one right now
How about...

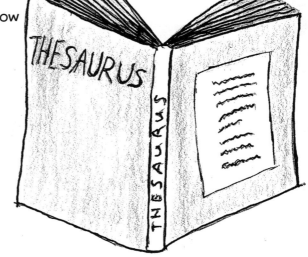

For Lease

This space for rent, got something to say?
This space for rent, two bucks a day.
"House for sale"
"I'll fix your car"
How about a picture
of a movie star?
"God loves you"
"Save the whales"
"This get-rich-plan NEVER FAILS!"
"Show me your palms – I'll tell you your fate"
"Look better in days-lose half of your weight"
What would you say if this was your space?
What would you say if you were in my place?
Me – I'm outta' lines so go take some space.
Then take a little time-it's never a race.
Put on some paper what you grab from the air.
Don't strain too hard...
It's already there.

George's Typewriter

George's typewriter is one mean machine.
Its old witchy fingers are long and they're lean.
They stamp the paper with a click and a clack.
Its ribbons pulled taut, not one ounce of slack.

The old round black keys tapping out a song,
with nothing considered grammatically wrong.
With no fancy screen, nothing hi-tech–
it would never dream of a built-in spell check.

It knows how to spell, thank you very much.
It knows how to punctuate, abbreviate and such.
It knows proper nouns from their commoner kin.
It knows the double negative is an unforgivable sin.

It treats participles well, never dangles them from
an incomplete sentence or clause left undone.
Prepositions are safe in its old, steady keys.
Unclear modifiers are brought to their knees.

It has synonyms for each nuance of meaning.
All adverbs are given a well deserved screening.
Adjectives are used but not overly so.
Powerful verbs are what makes its dough.

The letter of the law has its part but it's clear,
the spirit grabs the heart when it pleases the ear.

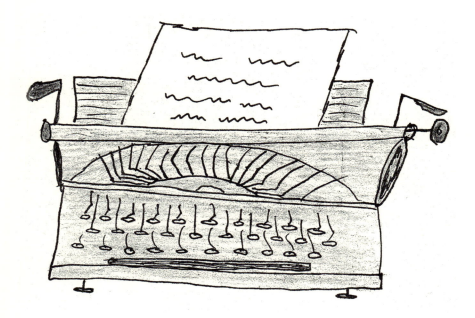

What Writers Know Best

Some think they have secrets
passed down from heaven,

or they're luckier than a horseshoe
or old number seven.

Some think they know better
about how things work,

about the angels that watch us
and the monsters that lurk.

Some think the words flow
into a best selling caper

but what writers know best
is crumpled up paper.

The Loveliest Couple

Which two words make the loveliest pair?
Surely it isn't "under" followed by "wear."

Which two words sound the best together?
How 'bout the phrase "summery weather?"

I like when the word "hot" found the word "dog,"
or when the word "cabin" is preceded by "log."

Mom thinks there's magic in Dad's old "love letter."
I know there's magic in "twinight doubleheader."

Who doesn't love "day" with the word "dream?"
But the best is the day when "ice" met its "cream."

The Little Girl Who Eats Her Words

I know a little girl who's been eating her words
since she was six months old.
Before she could talk or read or walk
she believed what she was told.

Any piece of paper that came her way
went straight into her mouth.
The paper got gummed and rolled and chewed
before it headed south.

When she got older and found her voice
it came as a surprise —
the first words that would pass her lips
were "Tomorrow sunny skies."

Then she talked about some stocks and bonds
and a well-past baseball game.
She told a story about an actress
from Hollywood movie fame.

And ingredients to a recipe
and directions to the place
they had visited a year ago
that were left too near her face.

Every word that she had eaten,
every line that she had chewed,
she spat back out for all to hear
as if spitting up her food.

So if you are a writer of words
write what's good, or better, best.
You never know exactly what
a young reader might digest.

What Was Left on the Ground

I knew a hundred stories
were lying on the ground.

I heard a thousand songs
that didn't make a sound.

I saw a dozen pictures
at least twelve thousand words.

I felt a million poems
dying to be heard.

I wish that groom had written
his love down for his bride.

I should have picked that pencil up
to see what else inside.

A Poem is a Little Child

A poem is a little child
of smaller frame and mind.
The truth of which is not so mild,
nor easily confined.

Something of a timeless story,
something of a hymn,
something hiding boundless glory
bursting from within.

Something of a victory,
something of a wild ride.
Every part a mystery
hidden deep inside.

Big Words

A person's big vocabulary
is like a nation's arms.

You feel more secure knowing they're there
should someone wish you harm.

With a large stockpile of either one
you must always be wary

of never assaulting anyone
unless gravely necessary.

I See a Story...

When I shut my eyes and the world is black,
a little something always stares back.
A word or a phrase,
a story or a rhyme
tries to get through
most every time.
And when my eyes open
what do they meet?
They spy a story
falling at my feet.
I see a story in a bristling leaf
and one under water
by the coral reef.
I smell a story in a cup of tea.
I hear another
in the buzzing bee.
A Christmas tale spins
when the wind starts to blow
I see a story
in how the pine needles grow.
So what is your story,
what is it you do?
Me-I see stories
and I see one in you.

Help Me End This Poem

Do you know a word that rhymes with "poem"
so I can end this verse?
This line is simple since I can rhyme it with
"adverse", "converse" or "terse."
But it's so very hard to find a word
to end the line after "poem."
I'm sure there are ten or twenty such words...
but I sure don't know 'em.

Other Things...

Other Things

The grown-ups worry about everything,
money, clothes and cars.
"Will we ever have enough?"
"Let's shoot for the stars!"

Grown-ups see what's in their sight-
the schoolhouse bell that rings.
The kids inside the schoolhouse know
that there are other things.

Grown-ups explain the rainbow's colors,
their sense for that is keen.
But we can sense a deeper meaning
behind just what is seen.

Grown-ups know of presidents,
but we know queens and kings.
Grown-ups learn to rule the world
but we know other things.

The Why-Nots

Have you ever met the Why-Nots?
Look—they're all around.
Just say you have a good idea
and they pop out of the ground,
to tell you why it can't be done
and why you musn't try,
to tell you that it's nothing more
than pie up in the sky,
to tell you why not and "heavens no"
and "absolutely NOPE,"
to squash your dreams and hand you fear-
erase all trace of hope.
"This is why not, this is why not!"
"This is why it can't be done!"
So when you hear the Why-Nots,
just shut your ears and run;
or better yet look to the sky
and they'll vanish in thin air.

'Cause hopes and dreams come from above
and Why-Nots can't live there.

What's In Your Safe?

What do you have hidden?
What have you stocked up?
What is it you've stashed away?
What have you locked up?
What is that inside your safe,
 safe from searching eyes,
 safe from restless hearts,
 safe from cloudy skies?
Maybe it's a picture
painted from your heart.
Maybe it's a story
or some such work of art.
Maybe it's a memory
you won't let see the day.
Maybe it's a joyful thing
you've let be put away.
Maybe it is something dark
that now needs to be bared.
Maybe it's some sort of light
which means it must be shared.
Maybe it is something old,
 maybe it's quite new.
Open the safe and give it away –
 the precious thing is you.

How High You Can Go

Losing your way is like digging a hole;
it gets a lot darker, the further you go.
The further you go, the less you can see;
the less you can see, the darker you'll be.

But while you are digging straight into the world,
there is a place where your dirt gets hurled.
And the deeper you've fallen, the higher the mound,
the higher you can climb...

if you just turn around.

Angel Sight

There is a little girl
with the strangest sight.
She sees only light
in the middle of the night.

When there's four in the room,
she sees eight.
When she's all by herself
she talks to a mate.

This girl can see angels,
if you only knew,
the one watching, waiting
she sees next to you.

Something Lost

St. Anthony, St. Anthony come around.
Something's lost that can't be found.
I lost my temper again today.
This time I lost it all the way.
So when you find it, let me know.
Then wrap it up in ribbon and bow.
And give it to Jesus, humble and meek.
'Cause I'd just lose it again next week.

Poor Clare

Poor St. Clare
ain't poor no more.
She'll be livin' good
forevermore.

'Cause now she's as rich
as she could be.
Her investment paid off...
heavenly.

My Financial Planner

Invest in stocks, buy some bonds.
Consult the current interest rate.
Buy it low, sell it high.
Hold on to some real estate.
A mutual fund, a treasury note,
adjustable loans,
numbers that float.
Diversify, multiply,
compound every day.
Dividends and higher yields;
a job with higher pay.
Modern day barns to store all our stuff
at the National Bank of Never Enough.
My financial planner has taught me to say
Just give me enough
bread for today.

The Right Time

CALENDAR	
TODAY	TOMORROW
What is it you need to do? Ask yourself right now. Don't talk about the thing called "when." Just start in on the "how." Now, I tell you, is the only time, later is for bums. Tomorrow isn't even promised you and someday never comes.	
NEXT TIME	LATER ON
SOMEDAY	NEVER...

The Way Things Happen

I thank God for sunny days
and days when my team wins.
I thank God for laughter and
giggles, smiles and grins.
I thank God when I do well,
no errors and four-for-four.
I don't really like so much
talking to a bore.
Or rainy days
or losing games,
or going 0-for-five.
But those things, I've noticed, happen too
as long as I'm alive.
I hate when pens explode on me
and dinner gets burnt to ashes.
And why is it I never know
just where the secret stash is?
I can't stand losing
(as I said before)
that feeling never ends.
And don't you know it's twice as bad
in a game against my friends.

I simply loathe when the power goes out
and all my ice cream melts,
or I'm running late and my pants are too big
and I can't find any belts.
I abhor all traffic and rain delays,
all house and forest fires.
Oh how I burn just thinking about
my bike with two flat tires.
Well I do thank God for Saturdays
and turning five bucks into ten.
But saints thank God for bores and rain...
and the way He lets things happen.

The Dangers of a Well-Fed-Big-Head

I've worn the horns of the goat who lost the game
and survived it all
just the same.

I've been raised in praise with the victor's wreath
and only survived that
by the skin of my teeth.

Put Together Right

Jesus was a carpenter
long before He made me.
But something went wrong
apparently.
You see I've been told
I'm missing a bolt.
I don't know which one
so it can't be my fault.
And then it seems
I have a loose screw.
(And some people say
I likely have two.)
And once it was said
that my head's not on tight.
So it seems I just wasn't
put together quite right.
But I see no loose screws
or bolts that aren't there,
or heads that are loose
underneath all my hair.
And my carpenter is good,
no ifs, ands or buts.
So maybe,
just maybe,
everyone else is plain nuts.

The Ballad of Wasted Time

There's a sad song they say
that everyone sings,
from the idle-weary pauper
to the greatest of kings.

Who can stand to answer
for time frittered away?
Who has never wasted
a single, sacred day?

Who will ever know
the value of each hour,
or heed the awful warning
of the terrible bell tower?

You can take your wasted time
and make it bless our King,
Who will turn a sad song into joy –
right now His praises sing.

Beneath Her Mantle

Every sun must rise with a prayer
which colors days like light through air.

Each sun must be put to bed
with the words that we, as children, said.

And in between let's drop some hints
that we walk and sleep in confidence.

Beneath a motherly sky of blue
which brings the sun to me and you.

St. Michael's Army

When my eyes are shut tight
and my sight is clear,
I can see traps set here
and dragons there.

As they creep in the night
I never fear,
because I see angel warriors
everywhere.

Hidden Gold

I've found the sum of all men's wonder
I've met the God of sun and thunder.
I know what they yearned for in hymns of old.
I've cased the rainbow and found the gold.
I've found the city lost in the sea.
I've trapped a leprechaun and the tooth fairy.
I've dined with Santa at the North Pole.
I've found the treasure the pirates stole.
I've tasted the magical potion of truth.
I've bathed in the waters of the fountain of youth.
I've battled the bogeyman
and the monsters of the deep.
I've woken the sandman from a deep winter's sleep.
I've ridden the neck of the beast in Loch Ness.
I've won the favor of the beautiful princess.

Every single dream man has dreamt in his head,
is but a fainting shadow
of my Angel's Bread.

A Little Advice

There are advisors everywhere.
Some give advice because they care.
Some advice is like a ray
of sunlight on a cloudy day.
But most advice is not that way...
and you need not listen
to what I say.

Eve yone's Mis ing Som thing

I know a boy, Tommy is his name.
He's missing a leg,
but he's always game.
He moves on his crutches
on walks short or long.
I don't know anyone
whose arms are so strong.
And little Suzy Mae
has the hardest time
pronouncing her words
but that is no crime.
Because you should see
the pictures she paints,
as clear as the light
on the halos of saints.

Benny can't see the clock,
Betsy can't hear the bell,
but together they perceive things
five times as well.
And then there's small Audry
who can't walk, talk or play.
What do you think she'll find
that day?
When she runs into God's house
and looks into His eyes
and sees all her treasures
with the thrill of surprise.
Preserved with His love,
handed back at His door,
things that were missing
will be missing no more.

Daring

Be daring because it's meant for you.
Be daring because the daring are so few.
Be daring even if no one understands.
Be daring just to prove you're in His hands.
Be daring and never be afraid.
It's the compliment Love must be paid.

Glimmers

The chorus of childhood,
"I can, I can."
That blessed refrain,
"Do it again!"

A grit of the teeth,
"Let me try!"
The search for truth,
"Why, why, why?"

No ideas or passions
hidden inside.
No smile not smiled,
no tear uncried.

The invisible God
all earth can hail
in a child's face—
Its thinnest veil.

Summer of the August Queen

In the summer months we dig out weeds.
And there we plant our May-flower seeds.
We watch and water our garden's soil —
for fruits to rise from all our toil.
We won't see colors until the Spring
when showers fall and new birds sing.
I know not what these flowers be,
the seeds fall from a sad, old tree.
Little miracles-all thirty-one,
bloom every year at May's first sun.
One flower for every day in May,
we pick each morning as we pray.
Our tree points with a nodding lean
to the statue of the august Queen.
There we lay the flower each morn
at her feet beneath that heart once torn.
The tree repeats his yearly tune
and drops his seeds at the first of June.
We work all summer until September.
What does that sad, old tree remember?

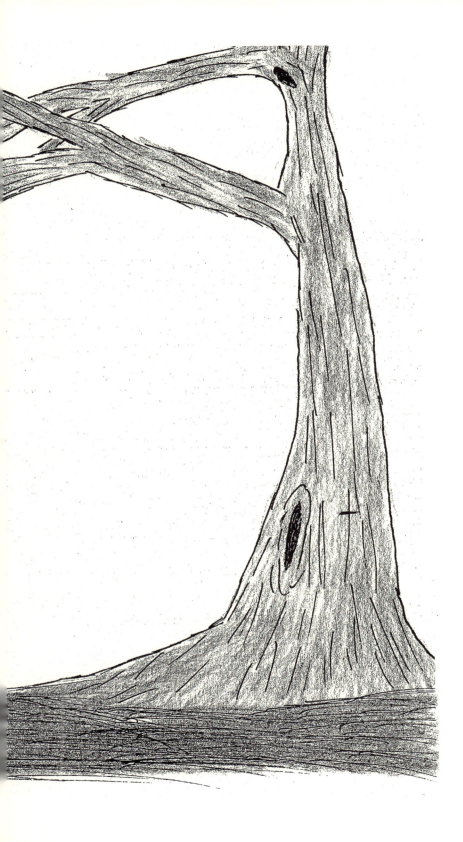

Christmas Song

I believe in Sunday nights
and Tuesdays just as well.
I believe in stories told
and stories left to tell.
I believe in Angel's Bread
and blessings in the sky.
I believe in daydreamers
and giving it a try.
I believe there's magic in
the thrill of Christmas Eve.
Wonder, dreams and miracles,
in these too I believe.
I believe in wild geese
and poems that can sing.
I believe in Christmas Day
and the Child born a King.

The Picture Comes Clearer

If I could paint that picture
I have inside my head,
it would be a children's poem
with no word left unsaid.

If I could leave you something,
it would be a hopeful dream,
the faith of little children
in things as yet unseen.

The picture comes still clearer
while the spirit still grows young,
and children never look back
while songs are left unsung...

Acknowledgments

For all their help in preparing this book,
my sincerest thanks to Katie Hubley, Olga Fairfax,
Rebecca Humrich at Sheridan Books and especially
Suzette Perry at Infinity Graphics.

For inspiration that was as free as it was priceless,
thank you David and Julie Spagnolo.
You guys are no "Why-Nots."
The idea for "The Mailbox" was conceived through the
generosity of Bert Keys.
The idea for "My Favorite Things" came while thinking
about one of my favorite people, Johnny, the
original #22.
It would be a sad "Backyard" without the Mallory clan –
JoAnne, John Paul, Magdalena and Joseph.
The inspiration for the better portion of the book
came from my precious "Sleepfighters" –
Gracie, Rose and Lucy.
You are true poems.

For all the rest,
blame me.

Cover design and layout by Suzette Perry

Thank you, Mom

and thank you, Dad,

for the childhood

I had,

which through these pages

shines right through.

Truly know,

you wrote them, too.